My Filipino Parents' Worst Nightmare

The Dela Cruz Sisters

Chey Caliso

Main Characters

Jaslene Maria Dela Cruz - The main protagonist but is considered the demon child to Lisa and Oscar.

Amalia Dela Cruz - Jaslene's supportive sister who is currently attending University.

Lisa Dela Cruz - Jaslene and Amalia's mother. Jaslene doesn't get along with her mom because Lisa cannot stand the way Jaslene's mindset is which causes them to argue multiple times throughout the story.

Oscar Dela Cruz - Jaslene and Amalia's father. He tends to follow Lisa's orders which frustrates Jaslene.

Angel - Jaslene's best friend who has supported her all the way.

Gia - Jaslene and Amalia's aunt (Oscar's sister) who is a lot more open minded than their parents and welcomes them to their home any time.

CHAPTER 1

My parents sure lived the American dream alright. That is before I was born. Once I came along, they started to feel miserable again. It started off with me being born as a girl. They wanted one boy and one girl and there is already Amalia who is their favorite child to begin with. She can sing, is a devoted Catholic, is studying nursing and even agrees to save her virginity until marriage and not date until after college.

I actually believe that knowing her but imagine if she turned into some wild college girl who forgot about praising the Lord and just occupied her time doing hookups along with changing her major to dance, something she also loved doing but mom laughed in her face when she said she was considering it. Her three majors in mind were dance, nursing, and filming. The second reason why she chose nursing was because mom "convinced" her. Toxic fucking bitch.

Anyways, their dream of having a boy failed. Three years before I was born, my mom suffered a miscarriage. They never told me, I had to learn that from my cousin at ten years old so I asked my mom if it was true, but she never answered back.

What was wrong with me according to them? I don't believe in God, I always had the dream to be a writer, I don't speak Tagalog and I'm bisexual. To them, my sexuality was the biggest taboo.

My parents came to this country at twenty-eight years old, a month after their marriage. Once they came here, they thought they were going to live a perfect life and have the perfect family. They met in grade school and ever since they started dating and they both had this goal to come to The United States but somewhere where the Pinoys are at so they thought they wouldn't lose the culture.

Back in the Philippines, my parents lived in extreme poverty. They were only able to afford rice and eat the fish that my uncle and his friends caught. They lived in the capital Manila and it was very crowded. Many lived in a one bedroom apartment with up to ten people living there, others might live in shacks with a few different families. If you didn't have that option, then you probably would be on the streets or maybe even living in the cemetery.

I've watched videos on the poverty of the Philippines, especially those who were living in graveyards. They all seemed happy that they had somewhere to go but I was deeply upset for them. I made a promise to myself that once I became a rich writer that I would do something to help the people in my country and other countries as well. As of right now, I can only spread news articles and do volunteer work around my community because I'm broke living off of Journey's money.

Once my parents came to America, my mom went to school to become a nurse practitioner while my dad went to school to become an engineer. With the amount of money they made they were able to reach all of the other goals they had which mainly had to do with traveling. Together they went to Hawaii, Canada, Mexico, Germany, Puerto Rico and even went back to the Philippines just so we could meet the family.

My mom doesn't want to take me there anymore. She knows how rebellious I am which can't be tolerated back home. It's always respect the elders no matter what but I, Jaslene Maria Dela Cruz, will not tolerate disrespect. Just because I'm only sixteen does not give you the right to talk down on me.

I've gotten in trouble for talking back to adults but they just don't get how you can't treat kids like that. One time my dad's friend said, "Blonde on Filipino women is reserved for hookers

with a cheap rate, so Oscar keep track of what your kid is doing."
So I replied with, "why should my father worry about me when
your son has to go to the Emergency Room twice a year to get his
stomach pumped?" Everyone in the room was shocked and I had to
have a talk with dad when he was driving home that night.

"Jaslene, you can't say something like that!"

"He started it." I snapped back.

"It was a joke, learn to take one."

"It wasn't funny."

"Well, the next time we see him, apologize!"

"Why should I have to apologize? He disrespected me first
and it was racist!"

"Jaslene, you just don't say that to someone older, you went
too far. It was also not meant to be taken seriously!"

Once we got home that night, I locked my door because I
was scared of what my mom was planning to do. My parents were
both speaking in Tagalog which I only caught onto bits and pieces.
My parents never taught Amalia and I because they felt like it was
useless since everyone in the family knew English so it wouldn't
be a problem to communicate with them. Once we got older, they
then realized how much they regret it and are now frustrated that
we cannot speak the language when they had the opportunity to
teach us during our whole childhood.

After that night, I didn't come out of my room for the
whole weekend. When I had to leave for school on the following
Monday, my mom slapped me on the face so hard. It wasn't even
my fault, it was dad's stupid friend's fault. If he didn't make a
comment on my blonde hair I wouldn't make a comment about his
son.

I dyed my hair blonde at fourteen years old after I got
dumped by someone I really liked. It's an ABG thing. We do this
thing where when we go through a hard time like a break up, we
just end up going through a blonde hair phase. I ended up liking it
on myself, so I decided to keep it.

I was a freshman in high school when I first started dating

Gabriel, he was sixteen. I lost my virginity to him because he kept persisting and I agreed because I really liked him although I wasn't ready. The first time sucked. It hurt, he was sweating all over me, and his bed was uncomfortable! Then two weeks later he broke up with me because he had feelings for another girl who was in his class.

The day he broke up with me through text, I decided to have a self care day with my best friend. We got my hair colored, got pedicures and watched Total Drama Island on Netflix. I got over it three months later.

Once him and his girlfriend broke up due to her cheating, he wanted to hook up with me again before he went to college.

"I'm now in a relationship, but even if I was single, I'd still say no. You were the worst sexual partner ever."

I definitely hit a nerve because he then ranted about how Filipina women were not wife material but only good for hookups. Like sir, you're half Filipino. I'm not surprised he is in a frat, Alpha Apple Pie or whatever the fuck it's called.

CHAPTER 2

I don't remember the last time my mom and I exchanged an "I love you." I can't handle how toxic she is. Amalia and her get along so much better. Mom and dad call her Angel or My love while the only nickname I get is JJ.

I hate how my mom wants to control my beliefs and lifestyle. She says I have to be a nursing major but I'm passionate about being a writer, she says my sexuality was a choice, and that Atheists have mental problems. I mean I do but it's not because of that.

Once I came out to her as bisexual, she called it a phase and said that a daughter having a girlfriend will not be accepted in this house. I told this to her at fourteen and now I regret it. I should have kept it to myself because sixteen-year-old me is thinking why should I tell my family what I'm sexually attracted to?

She thinks she is allowed to control who I date. I get that parents want someone who is good for their kids, but she is going at this the wrong way. She has to approve who I date but if I let her then I might as well get with someone who I don't love. She wants someone so different from what I ask for. It's my fucking life!

I feel like she should be grateful I'm dating a girl, at least I can't get pregnant! I'm glad that my cousin, Mel, is accepted by my Tita Gia. Gia is my dad's older sister. Mel came out to her parents at seventeen and Tita Gia always made sure to make her feel comfortable and wanted to protect her as much as she could.

When we first heard about Mel being gay my mom

wouldn't stop chismising about it. She pointed out the stuff she would wear was "not gay" at all. She believes that the LGBT community has a stereotypical way of dressing which is the way that Mel happened to look after coming out. Once she came out to everyone, she changed up her fashion style and cut her hair super short that my mom wasn't a fan of. Me on the other hand, I was glad to see Mel happier and more comfortable with herself.

Mel is in college now and goes to a very liberal school in Washington, D.C. My mom says she has perfect grades, goes to a great school, and is a talented piano player but mentioned it was a shame for her to be gay. It pissed me off so much when she said that that I ended up not finishing dinner, so I went upstairs and locked my door. My mom's homophobia makes me cry every time from frustration.

*

Gia studied Arabic in school so she could eventually work in Dubai and become the breadwinner in my dad's family. The woman had to support six people with the money she made. She's part of the reason why my parents were able to reside in Texas. Respect to her.

Since I don't feel loved by my parents, Tita Gia made me feel like I was her own kid. She would let me stay at her house whenever I needed to, fed me well, and would give me great advice. My mom and her friends always made fun of me for having darker skin, but Aunt Gia would tell me I'm beautiful no matter what. It's interesting how mom bullied Amalia and I for having darker skin yet she made us. Not even that but she also had darker skin as well, like my complexion but due to self-hatred she started getting her hands on skin whitening products.

As a child, my mom wouldn't let me go outside as much during the summertime because as they said, I'll be darker than I already was. Mom started calling me names like burnt and crispy which always made me feel sad. The person who created me started my villain origin story.

My mother's family had darker skin too but Lola used skin whitening products at a very young age and never told anyone but Lolo. I only found out when I was snooping around the house when I went back to the Philippines and found old photos of her and noticed the skin tone changed drastically.

"Lolo, why does she look different here?" I come to the kitchen and show the pictures.

"Your grandma was going to compete in a beauty pageant and wanted a better chance of winning and unfortunately for her that meant she had to change up some things. Her hair needed to be straighter and longer, she needed to be taller and had to lighten her skin. I always thought she was beautiful either way, but she cared so much what other people thought of her that she decided to go through all of those changes."

Lolo never had issues with his skin tone. He worked outside in the sun knowing that people were going to judge him but he didn't care because he liked his job and knew he was hard working. A lot of men didn't care, it was more of the women who cared about their looks.

When my mom was sixteen years old, she discovered Lola's skin whitening products. She was more open about using it though because she wanted to prove to her classmates that she could afford things when in reality, they struggled a lot when it came to money, but I guess skin whitening products was a need for them.

I once cried about my skin tone to Aunt Gia when I was five. There was a party at their friends house on a hot summer day where all the kids were playing tag outside so I wanted to join. My mom said no but I asked why the other kids were allowed to play and she said, "because even if they're in the sun, they won't get dark like you!" and started to continue playing mahjong.

Aunt Gia was eating on the couch and talking to her friend while I started bawling my eyes out. She said not to listen to my mom and that I can play tag with the other kids, so I did. My mom didn't even realize anyways because she was playing mahjong for three hours straight, desperate to win some money in the end. She did not win any money because of karma. As Kim Kardashian once said on Keeping Up With The Kardashians, "It's what she deserves."

My aunt came to the United States when she was twenty and lived in New Jersey where her husband is from but convinced him to move to Texas once my parents came so she can be with us who live fifteen minutes away. She supported mom and dad as much as she could but my parents don't seem to be as appreciative anymore honestly which I feel sad for her. Aunt Gia is my favorite aunt and deserves a lot of good things to come to her.

I told her everything about my life. The people I had a crush on, drama at school, how school was going, my sexuality and my religious affiliation. She took hearing about me being bisexual well, but she was perplexed when I told her I was an atheist. At first, she would try to convince me why God was real and try to prove to me why heaven and hell exists. Honestly, I didn't get any valid points, but I never judged her way of thinking and I thought she shouldn't judge mine. Fortunately for me, my uncle stepped in and convinced her that since my beliefs don't hurt anyone then I have a right to think that way, even though she had a hard time getting past it, she eventually did and we never spoke about it again.

A lot of my friends are atheists. We believe in science over God, but I am the only one who is confident to tell their parents what I believe in. They all care about making their parents happy, but my happiness comes first, so I don't care if my parents are throwing a fit about it each time they want to bring it up.

For this reason, it makes my mom have the urge to send me to the Philippines for a few years so I can get taught better with religion. Over here she doesn't like how the Catholics aren't good at practicing their religion. In the Philippines, they are more strict. Over here, the Catholics swear all the time but when you hear someone over there swearing, they gasp a lot of times. Swearing is considered to be a sin, but in the United States we just don't think about it deeply.

I wanted to live in The Philippines at first but then a traumatizing memory happened along with the bullying problems causing me distress. My friend was bullied so badly for being overweight that she resorted to homeschooling.

I went to the Philippines when I was twelve years old. I remember meeting a lot of family members, eating good everyday because man those mangos are good, playing with friends and going sightseeing. It was a good time until I met Gerald.

Gerald was fifteen years old when I met him and was a family friend. To the adults, they all looked at him as a nice sweet innocent boy but to me, I always knew him as Satan. When we were alone for the first and only time, he would always ask me sexual questions and half of the stuff he asked I didn't know he was talking about at the time. He then pulled me closer to him.

"Let's try this…" He then starts to go under my skirt.

"Please stop, I don't like this!"

"We only have to try it once."

"But I don't like it!"

I don't want to recall the rest. Just know it sometimes keeps me up at night especially when I didn't get justice for it. When I was ready, I told my mom why I didn't want to go back there. I was hoping she would understand this time, but she invalidated my feelings as usual.

"I was sexually assaulted by someone you guys knew! I'm never going back if he's in our house!" I cried.

"What happened?" she was concerned at first.

"I don't want to say, it was really gross."

"Jaslene, tell us!" she screamed.

"I'm only comfortable with saying that he touched me, you figure out the rest!"

"Well all I could ask is, what were you wearing?"

"Are you fucking serious? What was I wearing? You picked out my clothes for me until I was like thirteen!" I then ran upstairs because I just couldn't handle it anymore.

I always dress modestly because of the fear of being sexualized as an underaged girl. My dad's friends make me uncomfortable. They would talk about women so vulgarly, it didn't matter if they were under eighteen either, if they saw their cleavage or these girls wearing leggings, they were still going to point it out. These men were married as well. My mom would never let my dad talk about women like that though. She would easily deck him.

CHAPTER 3

I've been dating this girl for about two months now and she has already said "I love you." I might've made a white lie saying I love her too but I don't fully feel that way yet, my feelings are still developing. Last night, I was desperate for some moral support so I spoke to my best friend, Angel about this.

"She said I love you to me, it's only been a month and twenty-three days! I might have panicked and said I love you back and now I feel guilty." I say on FaceTime.

"It is a little early to say I love you but don't worry about it, you're going to feel that way soon." he said.

"It's not just that, she already invited me to the Bahamas during break."

"Shit! Well, are you going to take that offer?"

"I mean I want to go but I already know my parents answers."

*

Before dating Tanya, I never talked to her during school, all I knew about her is that she is seventeen years old and a lesbian. She randomly added me on Snapchat and we first started talking from there.

I didn't want to keep my relationship private, I was open to taking couples photos and holding her hand at school but I was worried about Ramona "Evil Snitch Bitch" Castillo. Our moms first met at church, I talked to Ramona a few times but didn't want to become friends with her because she happened to be homophobic and her only reason is because it's against Christianity. Which if there was a God, wouldn't God expect everyone to love each other no matter their sexual orientation?

Ramona and I go to the same school and we say hi but that's about it. My mom wants me to hang out with her more often but I don't think so. Her friend group are a bunch of Catholic pro-life douchebags. They protested at a Planned Parenthood a few times. Like please shut the fuck up, you won't change those people's decisions, you're wasting your time.

My parents know almost all of the Filipino students' families in my high school and I happen to be friends with a good amount of them, the ones who won't snitch on me to my parents anyways.

Only Ramona has bad intentions but everyone else, they mean no harm, it's that type of thing where they think my parents know but they actually don't because I keep secrets from them but I have my reasons you know. I drink a lot with friends which a lot of the parents will let them drink when there is an adult, but my mom would kill me if she saw a drink in my hand.

My mom parties a lot and there's always a bunch of alcohol. My friends and I would drink it in a separate room. I had my first drink at fifteen. I had a Bud Light which I ended up drinking four which I only felt a little buzzed, I definitely got that high tolerance of alcohol from my father. He had his first drink at twelve and he stole the San Miguel drink from some elderly German guy who owned the store with his twenty-two year old wife.

Five minutes after my second drink it was time for us to go home. I was able to walk fine but I refused to open my mouth. For the whole fifteen minute car ride home I was petrified she was going to find out so I pretended to be tired and faked being asleep in the car.

That was probably the only night my mom was okay to go

home. The other times she would be super drunk and we'd have to spend the night as she wasn't capable enough to drive. Ever since I started driving, she's made me drive home every time she was too drunk to drive.

13

CHAPTER 4

The first thing I felt when I woke up was my feet being grabbed. At first I thought it was a demon trying to attack me then I woke up and found out it was. My mother was the demon.

"Wake up!" she screamed in my ear.

"No, get out!" I go under the covers.

"You wake up now!"

"Get off me you psycho bitch!" totally forgetting that calling your mom a bitch is very low.

"What the fuck did you just say?"

"Now would God approve of your language?"

Every Sunday, she wakes me up at 9 AM for church, that is if I'm home. She had been doing the same routine since I was eight years old so two years ago I came up with a strategy. Have a sleepover at a friend's house on Saturday night so I can avoid church. I would always ask my father to take me before my mom gets home from work.

Before you ask, is church really that bad? Yes, yes it is. Everyone I've met there preaches the wrong thing and it just pisses me off. Like, I just have the urge to slap them instead of shaking their hand when we get into the "peace be with you" segment.

Now I don't think Christianity itself is evil but many people who practice it today have the wrong idea of it. Many Christians don't like gay people because that's what their God supposedly tells them but in reality, God would tell us to love others.

A month ago, one of the ushers was talking in the circle

after church that my mom happened to join. While my mom was talking to people, the usher asked if I had a boyfriend yet and I said, "No I have a girlfriend" and walked away. His jaw dropped.

My mom goes into the other room to talk to my dad. She's screaming at him about me telling me that I should go to church with them. My dad gave bottom energy so what is he going to do? He doesn't know how to give orders so you think Dad will help you in this case?

Although I have both parents in my life, my mom was the one who disciplined us, taught us everything she felt like she needed to, and took care of everything that had to do with school. It seems like my dad doesn't have a say in what my mom does with us but he claims that he just agrees with her.

I fell back asleep when I noticed my mom gave up on me getting ready for church. From sixth to ninth grade I was sent to a Catholic school, we had to go to mass every Friday then I would also go to mass with my family the following Sunday.

Fortunately, in the middle of my freshman year my mom noticed how bad my grades were getting and "threatened" to send me to the nearest public school. I had a D in every quarter in Math ever since fifth grade while I had average grades in my other classes.

My mom thought all public schools were trash and that the staff didn't care about the students, so she thought it was a great punishment. Once I went there, I realized how much better the staff treated us compared to those Catholic school teachers who were preaching against Satan while in reality, they were actually Satan.

Going to public school didn't really feel like a threat since the teachers were nicer to me and they cared about helping me with my homework. While being in Catholic school, I hated wearing crusty uniforms, I hated not being able to fill in my eyebrows with makeup, and I hated that I wasn't able to think freely. One time I made a joke to my friend about how I put the bible in the fictional section of my bookshelf not realizing the teacher was behind me and I got detention! It gave "go ahead and log out for me" energy.

I forged my mom's signature and told her I had to do
volunteer work for service hours. In Catholic school you get
detentions for the stupidest things. Wearing nail polish, your
cell phone going off in class when you forget to silence it, when
students hug each other or making those harmless jokes like how I
did.

I stopped believing in God at thirteen years old, when I was
in eighth grade. Prior, I used to pray every night to God but my
prayers were never answered so it made me think he couldn't exist.
Although things I did pray the most for in my past was for Liam
Payne to marry me, to be popular once I get to high school and to
have a Porsche when I can drive. I guess I only believed in them
all this time because it was forced from my family.

On a serious praying note, there were other times, mainly
once I turned twelve that I was thinking realistically. Like when
I wanted my cousin back home to beat cancer but unfortunately
that didn't happen and she passed away two weeks later at the age
of sixteen. Then the other time when I prayed for my one cousin
for her to get into her dream school, UC Berkeley but ended up
not getting in even though we all thought her records were good
enough.

At that point I just gave up with my own religion. It wasn't
only about the praying and how I never saw anyone up there
but also because I wasn't happy with other people from my own
community telling me that being gay is a sin.

It made me feel bad about myself. Once I attended a public
school, I met the right people. I was surrounded by other LGBT
people and allies as my friends. My best friend Angel is gay and
came out to his parents at twelve years old. His family didn't
accept it until recently.

Angel was the first person I met at school. We met in
science class and sat next to each other. The teacher would assign
class work to do with a partner and we eventually started talking.
We connected over our love for Lana Del Rey and The Vampire
Diaries. He was also the first person at school that I told that I am

bisexual.

"Jaslene it's pretty obvious." he said while eating a carrot at the lunch table.

"Really? How?" I asked.

"The peace sign in every photo of you and your obsession with Doc Martens." he joked.

"Interesting observation."

CHAPTER 5

My parents came back two hours later as they went out to eat with their church friends after mass. She walked past my room saying I was a disgrace to the family. At that point I was desensitized to it because I heard it so often but then today she had more than just that to say.

"I wish Jared was born instead of you!" she yelled outside of my room.

That was also the first time she mentioned his name to me. Not going to lie, that really hurt. I tried so hard not to cry but I just couldn't stop thinking about it.

Well, I'm not going to sit here and just cry about it in my room for the rest of my life. I'm feeling petty so I will go on that trip to avoid mom and dad. She doesn't want me around so I won't be around....temporarily.

I thought that maybe if I was gone then my mom would somewhat appreciate me. I say somewhat because she will never love me as much as Amalia. I'm not changing my mindset and pretending to be someone I'm not just to please her.

I called Tanya up to confirm my invitation for the trip and started packing my bags for The Bahamas.

CHAPTER 6

I blocked my mom's number during the whole trip and didn't even ask my dad if I could go. I just texted him "I'm going to the Bahamas with my girlfriend. I'll see you in a week." I noticed I was left unread before taking off. I'm going to be in so much trouble when I get home, but it will be worth it because I'm going to be drinking unlimited amounts of mango smoothies and swimming in clear water beaches.

Tanya, her two brothers, mom, dad, aunt and uncle are with us. They got separate rooms for the adults and kids which technically means we can do whatever we want! Since Tanya's oldest brother is twenty he bought us the drinks. We had shared a bottle of gin and rum and just talked about deep shit then fell asleep.

*

"Goodmorning JJ, hope you are being safe. I love you." was the text I woke up to from dad.

I have to admit, my dad is a better parent than my mom. Although he does act like a little bitch at times. He always follows my mom's orders given to us and does not say a word about it. When my mom went on a girls' trip for a week to Las Vegas and when she went to El Salvador for a month we had a lot of fun without my mom. Harsh I know, but he would spend a lot more time with us like how a parent should. He took us to the museum three hours away, but it was a museum that I always wanted to go to, he would take us out for ice cream every weekend, and would play with us outside.

I like that dad doesn't say crude things to me. He never has said "I wish Jared was born instead of you", he hasn't tried to force me to join the medical field, he never made me feel like a disgrace. It was all my mother. I want to work on my mother and I's relationship, but I just don't know how! She wants everything her way and that's the problem.

*

Tanya and I were spooning last night and it felt good in her arms. So far her brothers and cousins know we are a couple but to her parent's knowledge we are just good friends and that is okay, I want her to tell them we are together when she is most comfortable.

When I was fourteen, I briefly dated a girl from another school and even though we were together for less than a month, she wanted to be introduced to my parents, as a girlfriend although she knew I wasn't ready to come out to my parents. She kept begging me for three weeks to pressure me to come out to my parents which I couldn't handle so I just decided to break it off.

During that time, I was scared to talk to my parents about sexuality as it is looked at as taboo in our family. We are expected to only date to marry people of the opposite sex and have children with them. I can't predict the future and I don't know if I'll end up marrying a man or a woman. Whatever happens, happens.

*

We all went to the beach at around 10 AM. I wanted to get my tan on and the adults wanted to try some margaritas. Once they came back, Tanya's mom was talking about how she's planning a trip to Mexico in two summers so her family could reunite

20

again. Mrs. Channing even invited me and I was surprised but I'm definitely down to go.

She is from Morelia, Mexico. It is known for historic buildings and cathedrals which you would think that it really isn't my thing. Which it's not but a vacation is a vacation and any opportunity to get away from my parents I will take. I do prefer to be in Cancún but I believe I will also have a good time in Morelia as well.

*

Two hours later, we went back into our hotel rooms to prepare for the boat tour her aunt had scheduled. I was the first one to go in the bathroom and I already noticed that I became two shades darker than I already was. Now I like getting tanned because I thought it looked good on me, but my mom thinks it doesn't. My mom was big on her skin lightening products, she would make it known that she would use it because it showed people that she somewhat had money.

Even though it can get humid in Texas, I wasn't outside that much, I also naturally had tan skin. Even without my tan, I'm probably one of the darkest Filipino children in our community of Filipinos that my family knows.

When I was in sixth grade, I did plan to get skin whitening products when I got older due to my mom and her two friend's mean comments. Once I got to my freshman year, I learned to love myself. I started to notice the more representation that dark skin Asians had in the media.

In the Philippines, there are a lot of colorism problems. We see ads all the time over there that have to do with skin whitening. While these models showing it off thinks it harmless, it really does have an inordinate negative impact on our community. The Philippines has a diverse group of appearances. Some of us have fair skin while others have brown skin, some of us have big eyes while others might have more almond shaped eyes.

The Aetas are known to be the first inhabitants of The Philippines. They have dark skin, curly hair, and happen to be really short. They look the complete opposite of a Miss Universe Philippines. Both are beautiful but the problem is Aetas are bullied for their looks even though they are the first inhabitants of the Philippines.

Once colonization first happened from Spain, our country was never the same. My mom believes that my dad and her have Spanish blood but I secretly took an ancestry DNA test and found out that I didn't have Spanish blood so if they have it then it's very remote.

More than likely the only reason we have a Spanish last name is thanks to Narciso Clavería y Zaldúa. He is number seven on my hate list. I'm still working on adding more people but so far I have twelve names on the list.

My Hate List:

1. Gabriel - evil, in a frat, forgot to put deodorant the night he took my virginity, he smelled….salty.

2. Ramona - snitch, homophobic, pro-life motherfucker.

3. Charice - My mom's good friend who took part in bullying me as a child for my dark skin. Also a bitch to everyone she has ever met in her life, even her parents.

4. Kayla - This girl at my school who is obsessed with spreading the word of the Lord to non-Christians. I have told her to shut the fuck up and was proud of myself.

5. Sam - this guy in my science class last year who had a crush on me and would take my phone to mess around.

6. Ferdinand Magellan - Unsuccessful colonizing ass bitch.

7. Narciso Clavería y Zaldúa

8. Christopher Columbus - Ugly trifling bitch who sucks at geography more than the average American does.

9. Mrs. Revino - My fifth-grade teacher who would call on me in class when she was aware I didn't know the answer.

10. John - Dad's friend who made that comment about Blonde Filipinas are hookers.

11. Mr. Joteir - The first teacher who started my Catholic trauma. Satan can take on many forms and he lived within him.

12. Alan - this band kid who wouldn't leave me alone when I rejected him twice. He was ugly because he was pro-life.

 I usually call my mom's friends Tita or Tito first which means aunt but Charice made my childhood hell so she doesn't deserve respect. Also, just so you know, this list has no particular order. I just got bored in algebra class one day, so I started brainstorming random things and came up with this.
 I also hate algebra class and if Gabe Vanderstorm keeps talking about how I should be good at math because I'm Asian, I will beat the ever living shit out of him and make him throw up all the hot dogs he eats during lunchtime.
 Brb, I have to make a note that he also needs to be on my hate list.

*

 Tomorrow is our last full day in The Bahamas and I think I'm ready to say "I love you" but I mean it this time. Over the course of the few days being here I had such an amazing time and the people we met were wonderful. Tanya's parents are so nice and open minded, I feel jealous that I don't have parents like that.

While the adults in Tanya's family went to eat breakfast, we both went to the beach and cuddled together in a hammock. I was the first one to say "I love you" today and saying it before her for the first time made me so nervous but now I'm relieved.

CHAPTER 7

We boarded at 5 PM. During the whole flight I couldn't sleep. I was nervous to find out what's next to come. I'm definitely going to get my ass beat. This hasn't happened since I was ten and I still suffer trauma from it. One time my mom punched me so hard my nose started bleeding and she made me clean up the blood from the carpet once she left my room.

Another time was when I got a 30% on my science test and my mom found it on the website we had so parents could check our grades and my mom bolted in the room and slapped me right across the face.

My dad doesn't tolerate hitting so my mom didn't do it that often, only when I made a huge mistake and would only do it if dad wasn't home and if I snitched then she planned to do it again so I was afraid to tell him all the times she would hit me.

*

Mr. Channing helped me with my bags and then took off once I entered the garage. My heart sank when I saw mom's ugly ass orange Ford Explorer. I'm assuming by this time she is asleep. Before walking in, I unblock her number.

I walked in to see my mom on the couch with Snowball on her lap. Snowball is my mom's ragdoll cat. She's a fucking demon. She sheds everywhere and kills every animal that comes across her, but my mom loves her more than me. I remember I got a white snake that lived in my bedroom. My dad thought it was okay since the cat never goes near my room and the snake was in a cage, but one day, the cat snuck into my room and managed to open the top. When I came back to my room, I saw my beautiful snake ripped into shreds. That's my most traumatizing memory. My dad cleaned everything while I was crying in the basement especially because I didn't want to see anything and my mom felt nothing and forgot about it the next day.

My mom loved animals when it came to cats, dogs, and rabbits but since she thought reptiles were ugly she didn't see them as a living thing and was okay with them dying. In the Philippines, she had three cats. She found them off the street. She couldn't afford to take them to the vet so their death would be expected when they got sick.

My mom got up from the chair to hug me. It felt uncomfortable honestly. Then after, I was getting yelled at. Not surprising.

"Do you know how much trouble you're going to be in? First off, you leave my sight, you're disrespectful and you have a girlfriend?!" she screamed.

"Mom, I really like this girl." I began to sob.

"Halá! I promise you, it's just a phase, one day you're going to find a good man, not now but in the future and marry that man."

"I can't predict the future. I really like this girl and I hope I end up with her but anything can happen. It's not a phase mom, I've felt this way ever since I started to feel attraction to people. So, around 7th grade."

She didn't say anything back, but she had the look on her face that intimidates the hell out of me. Once she took the cat back into her room, I went to my room and cried myself to sleep. Up until I was ten, we lived in a condo where I had to start sharing a room with Amalia because the third room was taken by my mom's close friend as she needed somewhere to live temporarily after a divorce.

We had bunk beds and I was the one on the bottom bunk.

Every time I would cry at night, mainly due to my mom, Amalia
would come down and sleep in my bed as well to make me
feel better. Although we are very different from each other, she
understands me. Since she has been away I have always missed
her. Now whose shoulder am I going to cry on?

*

Mom made us pancakes for breakfast. Probably because
she wanted to draw a frown with the whip cream into mine which
she only puts that for mine a lot. Everyone else would have a
smiley face on theirs.

"Real mature mom." I said.

"Oscar, do you know what she told me last night?"

"I'm sure it wasn't good." he continued to stuff his face
with the pancakes.

"Our daughter has been kissing girls! Do you have anything
to say about this?" She looks at my dad.

"Well it's not what I was hoping for but she's our daughter
and you have to let her be happy." Dad says.

"Mom, back in the Philippines you had a lot of gay friends
and you didn't treat them any different than your straight friends."

"Well, it's different when it's your kid. I want grandkids
and I don't want you to be discriminated against." she said,
frustrated.

"Amalia wants to have kids. Plus, I can still have kids by
adopting, which I would rather do anyways. I can't say anything on
the discrimination part, but I will be fine, I already know what to
expect and if someone physically attacks me, I have really strong
pepper spray."

My worst fear is getting pregnant. Did you know you
can lose teeth during pregnancy? I know that my parents want
biological grandkids but that is definitely not happening from me.
Ask Amalia.

27

CHAPTER 8

It's been three days since I talked to mom. To avoid her I've picked up four different people's shifts at Journeys. Sunday I worked a double, then Monday and today, I went to work right after school.

I called Amalia once I got home, I haven't heard her voice in three weeks. I needed someone to vent to as I wasn't feeling loved by the people at home. I tell her that mom has been not accepting of my sexuality and that I wished she cared about my feelings more. Being able to talk about this to someone feels good to release but it is stressful to go through this that I just end up crying from anger.

"I understand your pain Jaslene, so just give it like two hours. I'll talk to mom right now." she says.

*

While being on TikTok, mom walks into the room with cut up fruit.

"Your sister says I don't give you enough attention and I actually want to do better." she says. This wasn't like her at all, it felt weird.

"You can start by being more open minded."

"I am open minded!" she screeched.

"Then meet my girlfriend."

"If it will make you happy then I will."

"Wait really?" I questioned super hard.

"Yes. I will."

"Oh my god, thank you! Just please don't say anything foul."

"I will be on my best behavior."

I then hug her and she leaves for work. Hearing that didn't just make my day but my whole week. I probably owe Amalia big time for what she did. Like how did I win with my mom?

I asked Amalia what she said and she didn't respond until two hours later. She's always studying so it does take her a while to respond but it's reasonable. Even though the conversation started off as a screaming match, they then were able to work it out. She talked on the phone with mom which was a bit of a hassle, then talked about how even though my lifestyle is different than hers she has to accept it because I'm not hurting anyone and even though I have no religious beliefs it doesn't determine whether I'm a good person or not.

She tells her all of the good I have done in my life like when I threw a Spiderman birthday party for her friend's son and when I volunteered at the fish fry back in Catholic school, although I only did the one event out of the kindness of my heart. I just wanted free food at the fish fry because their food is so delicious. I had two plates full of food and even ice cream as well.

Volunteering for four hours was so worth it, at first I was just desperate for service hours because it was required for school but then I actually enjoyed the work there due to the food so I ended up volunteering every fish fry they had. It was honestly good to have something different to eat for dinner.

Everyday, my mom cooks breakfast and prepares dinner for us and it's usually pancit, tocino, lumpia and rice, or adobo which don't get me wrong, Filipino cuisine is appetizing, but I eat those foods way too much and I prefer to diversify my taste.

CHAPTER 9

I wish my situation would have happened after my mom agreed to meet Tanya, now I'm going to be embarrassed when I have to break the news to her. I broke up with Tanya last night after I left her house. We were cuddling on the couch and her phone started spamming with notifications. At first, I didn't think about it. I thought she was a trustworthy partner but since it started to annoy me how she was giggling at the notifications, I snatched her phone and found out it was Addison.

"What the fuck?" she screamed.

"No what the fuck is wrong with you, you told me you haven't talked since last year!"

"Well, we are just friends now."

"How long have you two been talking again? Be honest because I know when you lie."

"Like a month ago, but I didn't know it would bother you!"

"Before getting into this relationship, you knew my boundaries. I have to go."

Addison was her ex who she was in a serious relationship with from last year and told me she stopped talking to her after their breakup, so I'm more angry that she lied rather than her being an ex.

When Tanya and I were in the talking stage, I discussed a lot about my boundaries which I expected that to be ingrained in her head because she seemed worried about the consequences. I am in love with her but now I have to come to reality and realize that we aren't compatible no matter how much we love each other. During the talking stage, I didn't care if she didn't respect my boundaries but once we started officially dating, I hated when she brought up any of her exes or told me about the girls she hooked up with in the past. It started to bother me when she was friends with a girl named Kendra, a girl she would hook up with right after she and Addison broke up. I dealt with it before because I trusted her that their hookups were over.

Once I got home I made it known I unadded her on Snapchat because I wanted her to see the pending sign, but everything else I blocked her on.

I should've realized when I saw her following and the types of photos she would like on Instagram. It would be Instagram models showing their ass in G-string bikinis. Seeing that made me die a little inside but I didn't want to feel like I was controlling her. WHY DO ALL THE FINE ONES HAVE TO BE OBSESSED WITH INSTAGRAM MODELS AND BUYING THEIR ONLYFANS???!!! WE AREN'T EVEN EIGHTEEN!

During the talking stage, Tanya told me how she was hanging out with a friend and her friend bought this girl's OnlyFans and they started looking at videos to critique. I didn't mind it at the time because the feelings weren't as strong yet, but she did bring it up again a week after dating if she can buy this girl she liked from TikTok OnlyFans.

It wasn't something I was happy with so I calmly told her while being on Facetime that "I don't feel comfortable with you doing that." She tried to convince me one more time to let her do it but I said "If you do it, then enjoy being single" so she said that she wouldn't do it. Her mom also looks at her payment history every two weeks so I don't know how she would explain that to her mom. I guess to her, looking at OnlyFans of her internet celebrity crushes would be worth getting in trouble for.

A lot of people like to avoid the person they like following list but I just can't help it, if it's there I have to look and see what I'm getting myself into. Unfortunately, a lot of people follow

Instagram models and people they are so attracted to but what can you as their partner do about it? Nothing much but when she went to the doctor's office I was in the waiting room and she gave me her phone. I saw her type her passcode before so I was able to get in.

Going through her following list, she must have followed like twelve Instagram models. I unfollowed them all and I also unfollowed other people who went to our school that I didn't like. So I ended up unfollowing around one hundred people including Ramona. Her following list then became lower than her followers list so she probably would have noticed since she was on there quite a lot but she never brought it up with me.

Now that we are both single, she can follow whoever she wants now. Ever since I left her house angrily, I blocked her and she stayed blocked. I will not let my weaknesses let me unblock her just to see an updated following list. I wouldn't be surprised if she was following Addison though. Ninety-eight percent sure she did.

I'm upset about the breakup, but I guess I have to be grateful that I was able to go on a tropical trip with her and I didn't have to spend a single penny because her rich surgeon daddy and dentist mommy covered it. Even with souvenirs, Tanya paid for everything I wanted. A cute t-shirt, a mini Bahamian flag and a turtle plushie. With what she did to me I should have cleaned her out more. She has tried to add me back on Snapchat once but then I blocked it because now I know that she knows that I cut her off.

*

"Mom, you don't have to worry about Tanya anymore…We broke up."

"It's okay. Everything will be okay my baby." She then hugs me.

I didn't expect her to even care. I want to think more on the positive side, but I just have to assume the reason she's comforting me is because now her daughter has a chance to end up with a man again. I won't confront her because when I'm sad she actually gets me something that I really want.

"Is there anything I can do for you JJ?" she asked.

"Are you in the mood to drive?" I asked.

"Sure why?"

"Well, I would like the red, white & blue sorbet and frosted sugar cookies." I grinned.

"On it, I'll be back in less than an hour then."

"Ok bye."

CHAPTER 10

A perfect start to my Monday morning is seeing Tanya and her ex playing basketball together. After witnessing that, I'm trying not to ruin my mascara. During our time together, I never would have thought I was a rebound. Seeing that really triggered my soul.

This bitch really had to throw it away all for some ex who almost burnt the house down because she decided to leave the stove unattended to give her dog attention then totally forgot about it. I only know this because Tanya showed me the text messages of her freaking out.

"Tanya! The fire alarm is going off help!" along with two attachments of smoke filling the kitchen.

"Okay calm down." replied Tanya.

"Wait, did you even turn off the stove?" she double texted after realizing.

As soon as I got home I went right for my sorbet, took a spoon and ate it straight out of the box. My mom forgot her phone before going to work so you know I had to snoop. Honestly it wasn't that juicy when I saw the photos and her notes but the text messages…they were juicy but sadly not the good kind.

"If Amalia wasn't always bugging me about accepting JJ, I would have sent JJ to conversion therapy." She texts to Lola.

WHAT THE FUCK?! I thought I could go the whole day without ruining my mascara, but my mom succeeded. I ugly cried in the bathroom for an hour and Facetimed Amalia. She tried to calm me down the whole time but I knew she had an exam so I told her to take it although she mentioned she felt guilty.

I mean what can I do about it? It's not like she will send me since my strong ally sister, Amalia is able to annoy her with acceptance but I guess it just made me think of the other people as well who have been forced to go to conversion therapy by their parents. It's horrible and these parents act like being LGBTQ+ is a choice.

The most homophobia I've dealt with was from my own mother. I've had incidents where people would make aggravating comments like "it's just a phase", "girls kissing girls is hot" but then hope they don't have a gay son in the future, or a lecture from an older lady saying, "you will find the right man later in life and you'll stop thinking about these girls." Those sorts of things annoyed me but it didn't make me cry myself to sleep like how my mom's homophobic comments would.

I don't care how many times I have to tell my mom that I will always be bisexual. It was never a phase and it won't ever be. I'm sorry that I'm not the straight catholic church girl they always wanted me to be but at least I'm not doing things to put myself in jail. At least I'm not going out doing hard core drugs and shit, but she just doesn't appreciate me.

I'm planning not to date for a while, I don't think I can handle how complicated they can get so I'll just wait until after college. My goal in college is to play a lot of men, especially the ones in the fraternities but I don't want them to touch me, I'd rather have them use daddy's money to take me on fancy dinner dates then I ghost them.

I'm not even in college yet and I already know that I cannot stand fraternities. I'm convinced that it's a fucking cult.

CHAPTER 11

If I believed in God, I would blame them for testing me everyday. I made a promise to myself that I would avoid dating at all costs until after college. Well, I'm in class and I see the prettiest girl I've ever seen. She introduces herself to the class and tells us about her.

"Hi everyone, my name is Kaiya Mercado-Hansen. I was born in Oslo, Norway and moved to the U.S. when I was eight so we lived in Los Angeles until now." she says.

She kept saying more stuff but honestly that's all I remember because I wasn't even paying attention to her talking anymore. I was just mesmerized by how gorgeous she is. My red flag is that I go for the looks first then when I actually start paying attention to their interests and personalities then I start to lose feelings and/or I just can't stand their red flags, so I dip.

Everyone's red flags:

• Gabriel - followed twenty-three Instagram models which the majority were blue eyed white girls with crusty bleached hair. Oh, and he plays innocent girls.

• Girl from another school - pressured me to the point where it made me uncomfortable.

• Tanya - still talks to exes and moves too fast in relationships.

• Ashley - lowkey gave off microaggressions. For example, she would make comments about how good my English was and that I won't find other people like me in my minor. So yeah, fuck Ashley.

During lunch I had my chance to somewhat shoot my shot at Kaiya, so I decided to talk to ditch Angel for the day and make my way towards her as she was going outside.

"Hey, you're the new girl in my class. I'm Jaslene." I said.

"Hey, what's up?" She smiled.

I had no interest in this crusty school, but I pretended to just to get an excuse to be able to talk to her. She kept talking but once again I tuned out until I heard her mention how she likes slushies.

"Oh my god me too, you should totally check out Joe's Ice Cream shop. They serve ice cream of course, smoothies, and slushies." I said.

"Cool, maybe we can go someday?" she asked.

"For sure!"

"Cool! Well, I have to get to class but I'll see you later." she walks away.

"Bye!"

As I'm about to head back to the cafeteria, Tanya pops out of nowhere.

"Seems like you moved on quickly." She says.

"Chill out, it's not even like that and why do you care?" I snap.

"Maybe because I haven't fully moved on…."

"It seems like you did when I saw you on the basketball court with your ex."

"It's not like that either."

"Good to know but I don't care anymore." I walk away.

I'll admit, when we broke up I was hurt, especially when she didn't even seem to give a fuck. I thought I wasn't going to get over it for at least a month, but now I have someone else who can try to break me.

*

I had a stressful day at work. We are having a sale for this week so it's been the busiest we ever had. Our store is located at the end of the mall where no one really goes into the other stores. On a normal day we would probably only get like thirty customers while other stores get around two hundred.

Today we got about seventy customers. Many were going for the platform converse that was being sold for forty dollars for a limited time. I've dealt with two Karens so I tried my hardest not to get violent.

The first one was complaining how there was only one cash register and if I could hurry up scanning. She bought about five items, so I had to check if everything was accurate and her impatient ass was being ungrateful.

Then there was another woman with her husband. I swear the men who come with their Karens always get second hand embarrassment from them and you can just see in their eyes their dying to leave. Her problem was her ranting about how no one wants to shop here because it is so far to walk compared to the other stores people go to. She complained to us how we should move our store into the empty store by Justice. I told her "no we aren't going to do that Miss" because it isn't our problem and why should it only benefit her? These Karens always think the world revolves around them and someone needs to crush their dreams and it will be me.

I have gotten violent once. It was back at Catholic school when a bitch uglier than me called me ugly. I pushed her then she slapped me so I slammed her across the wall and was then caught by the teacher. We were then both in detention and we were forced to apologize to each other at the start of detention. Then once we got out the door I told her "I regret nothing."

I get my aggressive behavior from mom. I remember one time she had to draw a fifteen year old boy's blood and he wasn't cooperating well so she grabbed his arm and stuck the needle in

38

so fast and started collecting their blood. Mom wouldn't tell me this on her own but I found out from her co-worker when we had to give her a ride home and told us because she thought it was so funny.

*

"Who is Kaiya?" was the first thing mom asked when I walked in the door.

"How the fuck? How do you even know who that is?" I asked aggressively.

"Don't worry about it. Are you into her?"

"Chill out, you can't be asking me these questions and for all I know she could be as straight as that ruler on the table." I then go upstairs.

"Defensive ha?"

"Shut up!"

Once I graduate from high school I'm definitely going to school out of state. Recently, I've been researching on my MacBook for colleges. It might be too early to make a decision, but I can start applying for some scholarships. I have been thinking of going to school in Arizona or maybe Nevada. I'd like to go to The University of Arizona but if not there are many schools that seem nice in Nevada.

I don't have proof how I think I know how she found out about Kaiya but I'm ninety-nine percent sure it was from Ramona. I checked mom's most recent Facebook post and saw Ramona and her family eating from our hot pot from today. Sometimes whenever Ramona talks to me I imagine myself punching her because she just doesn't stay in her fucking place.

My mom barges into my room like usual and sees a suitcase on my bed.

"What is this?"

"I'm clearly not welcomed here, so I will be leaving for a while." I said.

"Stop this JJ."

"I saw your text messages between you and Lola, you would have been willing to send me to conversion therapy?" I bursted into tears.

"You had no right to snoop through my phone Jaslene Maria Dela Cruz!"

"You're right, but the stuff you said is disgusting, I don't think I can deal with it anymore."

I zip up the suitcase and head over to my friend, Sofia's house. Sofia has been my friend since sixth grade when I met her back in Catholic school. She is religious, but I am cool with her for not shoving it down other people's throats like how almost everyone else did at that school.

While heading out my mom tried grabbing my arm for me not to go but I refused to stay. She was screaming so loud that the neighbors could hear. One person even got outside the house to even see what was going on.

"Is everything good? Why is she screaming?" my neighbor asked.

"Everything is fine. Don't worry about me." as I wiped away my tears and went into the car.

The neighbor still stood there while I was pulling out and gave a shocked look at my mom. My mom went back inside and closed the garage door.

I blocked my mom and dad's number until I planned to come back. While being at her house I decided to help her mom with cooking dinner. They usually make Argentinian cuisine which I happen to enjoy a lot and would also like to learn how to make it myself.

As of right now, Sofia lives with her mother and grandma. Her brother is currently in college so she let me stay in his bedroom. Her father died three years ago in a plane crash when he had a business trip in The Netherlands. It was hard for everyone in their family to get over it and it took them months to stop crying about it.

After we ate choripán, everyone was tired and went to sleep. I couldn't sleep so I started working on some writing projects I felt like doing.

*

A lot of times I put my phone on do not disturb before going to bed. This morning I woke up to spam texts from Amalia. She was begging me to come home but I'm not going home until mom fixes what she did.

"Go home now, please Jaslene. She is so worried about you!" said Amalia's text message.

"No, there's a lot of things she needs to make up for." I replied.

"Jaslene… Mom has no idea where you're at. She's literally panicking."

"Why is she panicking if she hates me?"

"She doesn't hate you Jaslene."

"Her phone implies otherwise."

That was the last text message I sent as I had to get ready for school then I muted her messages. My toxic trait was that if I was being disrespected then I would always give the same energy which many of my titas couldn't understand. They thought my behavior was disturbing.

In the Philippines, my friends always respect their elders even when they are being made fun of by them. I would lose my shit so fast and come for their whole life if it were me in that situation. I have come for a few people before. One time Charice made a comment about how one of my classmates died and I said "yeah just like your ex."

She got so offended over the comment and started swearing at me in Tagalog. I don't get why she was mad when she started it. She only knew about a kid dying from my school because of Ramona. She didn't know how nice of a person he was and how he was battling a disease, but she would have still said it anyways.

So many people from school went to his funeral. I wasn't close to him at all, but we did talk a few times and he was really sweet. I even cried at his funeral. I was always hoping for him to live but unfortunately he passed away at the age of fifteen.

Charice is the type to actually wish death on people when she truly doesn't like someone. I hate a lot of people from my life, but I could never wish death on someone. So, we obviously know she wouldn't care about someone dying not until it comes to her family.

CHAPTER 12

I came back to Sofia's house with my mom and dad waiting for me. I didn't even see their car so I wasn't expecting them to be there at all.

"Jaslene, just please come home." says Dad.

"No I can't do that." I talked back.

"You will bring your ass back home Jaslene!" Screamed Mom.

"But you can't accept me for who I am, you even wanted me to go to conversion therapy." I started sobbing.

"Because being that way is a choice you decided to make!"

"No it wasn't. I've always been like this ever since I started to feel attraction to people."

"I can never accept this Jaslene."

"Fine then I'll just run away from home, I'll make sure you will never find me." I attempt to leave again.

"Get back here Jaslene." Shouted dad then I turned around.

"Look Mom, I have everything I ever wanted as in you gave me the items I want, the beautiful spacious home, and any food I wanted I was able to eat but something I didn't have was supportive loving parents, I would give up all what you gave me just for that."

Dad came in to hug me but mom still wasn't giving up on having a straight daughter.

"Lisa just accept the poor girl already!" said Mrs. Monzon while she was knitting a sweater.

"But I just don't like it!"

"It's not your life and this is your child. She is a hardworking sweet girl so appreciate that part about her."

"Thank you, Mrs. Monzon."

"Anytime sweetheart." She went back to knitting.

After that hell of a conversation, Mom and Dad talked in private in Tagalog but they were still in front of everyone in the living room. Too bad they include a few English words in most of their conversations so I had to somewhat hear why I shouldn't be accepted in this family by Mom unless there were changes.

My dad doesn't like it either, he also wishes I was straight but I can't control that and I have mentioned that to him numerous times. He's the one who will tolerate it more than my mom though.

After their quarrel, they finally told me I was coming home. They said it so calmly too. Mom went home separately while Dad drove the car I was driving. I still had tears running down my face, I kept trying to wipe it but it just kept going. I didn't talk to him and looked out the window the whole time.

We all got home at the same time and we didn't say a word to each other. We made eye contact when I was walking towards my room and that's when she threw the mug I made her in sixth grade across the kitchen and it shattered into pieces.

I was frightened because I was scared she was going to physically hurt me next so I ran as fast as I could with my suitcase and locked my bedroom door. Finally, Snowball was finally useful and happened to distract her by saying that she was hungry. Snowball is a fifteen pound cat who gets hangry if not fed every six hours.

CHAPTER 13

"Can you please come over?" I ask Gia on the phone as I'm weeping.

"Oh my god Jaslene, I'll be right there." she grabs her keys.

*

"Hala! Gia what are you doing here?" Mom asked.

"It was an emergency. Jaslene called."

"Oh don't give her sympathy!"

"She's actually hurt by you Lisa."

"Ate what's going on?" Dad walks out of the room.

"Asawa mo is terrible!" she shouted.

"Oh you didn't not just say that to me puta." They then almost got into a physical fight.

My dad came to the rescue and held down my mom from fighting her. I watched the whole thing until I decided to be noticeable and walk down the stairs.

"Stop fighting, your childish behavior is embarrassing Mom. You're the one who needs help more than I do."

I have Tita Gia come upstairs with me so we can talk in private. I tell her everything that has happened and she is in shock.

"This is horrible Jaslene, I wish you could stay with me." she said.

"I would rather live with your family than here. I don't feel comfortable here anymore." "It will be okay. Your Tita is here to fix this."

"Thank you." I said as she handed me a tissue.

As my parents have been ranting the whole time we were in the room together, Gia unlocks the door and goes downstairs. I watch outside to see what's happening and the first thing I notice is my dad holding mom's arms.

My mom has a tendency to get violent and has been in a physical fight with her brother once and dad had to come to the rescue. I believe that my mom needs therapy, but she thinks that she is completely fine and she also thinks it's a waste of money.

"Lisa, Jaslene has done a lot of good things in her life. You need to accept she doesn't have the same religious beliefs, that her sexuality is different and that she won't get an A in every subject. She works very hard in school, she's grateful for the items you gave her and she deserves your love too. If you can't treat her properly, she will be living with me from now on." She gave a lecture.

"There's so many things wrong with her Gia!" Mom screamed.

"There isn't. It honestly breaks my heart when I hear people like you say that bullshit, you're the reason I don't want you or people who act like you near my daughter."

Gia believes that it's important to get along with your family, but she was always overprotective with Mel because of her paranoia that she will be physically attacked just because she is gay. Ever since she found out my mom was homophobic, she didn't want to be near her as much and invited her over less.

"You can get out of my house Jaslene." she said calmly.

"What?" My heart drops.

"Honey…." my dad said to mom.

"You heard me." she turned emotionless.

Tears ran down my face again. Gia was there to hug me and we started packing my stuff. She had an extra room to use for the guests but decided to make it into my room.

While packing my dad was outside my room not saying

anything. We made eye contact and that was it. I knew he didn't want me to leave but he was too much of a coward to stand up to the tyrant Lisa.

Once Dad left, Mom started talking to Dad about what they should turn my room into. She had plans of making it into an office like room or a room for Snowball. She said it in English so she can make sure I hear every word to trigger me.

Once I left what was once home to me, I had to start thinking of how I could afford college. My plans were originally to go out of state, have parents pay for it, and go right after I graduate high school. My new plan is to now commute to a closer college, take a gap year so I can work then attend University.

Gia wants to adopt me, it's not for sure but she has been thinking about it. It's the biggest change I'll ever go through and I just have so many mixed emotions. I would love for her and Uncle Ron to be my parents but I still love my dad no matter how messed up it was for him to follow my mother's footsteps. I have the heart to one day forgive Dad but I don't think I could ever forgive Mom.

10 Of The Most Messed Up Shit Mom Did To Me:
1. Has this urge to send me to conversion camp.

2. Made fun of me for being dark.

3. Told me to go to hell because I didn't want to go to church.

4. Told me to kill myself.

5. Implied it was my fault for being sexually assaulted.

6. Kicked me out of the house.

7. Beat me when I yelled at her to stop texting while driving.

8. Forces me to go to church even though I'm an atheist. Like I

don't spread what I believe in to her.

9. Screams "I hate you" to me when she doesn't get her way.

10. Wishing her son was born instead of me.

CHAPTER 14

This past week has been stressful. I've been packing and unpacking, cleaning non stop and having to cook for the four of us. Gia likes my homemade Chipotle meals and asks me to make it a lot and since she saved me from homelessness I had to agree.

This is the first day in five days I have gotten some freedom. Last night Kaiya asked me if I wanted to go out and smoke with her but I was just so tired so I asked if we could get slushies that would be planned for this evening. She agreed and will be picking me up tonight.

*

She picked me up in her Mercedes Benz. I think I know her red flag now. Spoiled rich girl. I don't necessarily look for partners with rich parents. It just naturally comes to me. Gabriel's family owned Teslas and Tanya's mom is a dentist while her dad is a surgeon so you can already imagine how nice the house must be especially since you can get a big ass house if you have those professions here in Texas.

While I got into the car I noticed we were wearing somewhat similar outfits. So it has to be that we are meant to be soulmates. Just kidding. I wore my black converse platform shoes, a red cotton tank top while she wore white converse low tops and a pinkish-reddish satin tank top.

I ordered a banana slushie while she had a cherry one. We

took aesthetic pictures for Instagram then sat down on a bench talking about life.

She likes tarot cards, going to the movies, working out, and going to poetry slams. The total opposite of what I like.

Tarot cards aren't my thing, I hate watching movies, just going there and sitting in the same spot for more than an hour triggers my soul. I don't like working out, and poetry slams are just not my thing but I would be down to go to see if I can get some inspiration from something.

When you have a crush on someone, you want to find the things you have in common with them and we still haven't gotten anywhere yet. Hopefully we like the same music.

"I'm really into Eminem, Machine Gun Kelly and Halsey."

Nevermind. I don't think we can find anything in common. Maybe she just has a great personality that I get to fall in love with later on. I still have hope. If I only like her for her looks then I'll just leave but if I can develop feelings within the first two weeks of us dating, then I would like to have something long term.

As you can see, I'm very impatient. I date to marry, not to play around and waste time. It's amazing how others do it but not me though.

I also take marriage very seriously, so it's important to choose the right person to marry. I'm not a Kardashian where I can horse around with marriage. A red flag about me is that I'm worried about the money. Weddings are expensive then imagine if I get divorced two years later like my tita. After her divorce she started dating a new guy then married him so my cousin started her speech off with "Welcome to round three, this is the second out of the third wedding of my moms I have attended." This happened four years ago and I remember it vividly. Many of the guests laughed, others jaw dropped and others had the look of second hand embarrassment on their face. Her mother had the death stare right after that comment.

She did not like that and once we all went back to the hotel room, her mom screamed her system out the next five rooms could hear. My tita and her third husband are still happily married and I think they will last.

*

Tita Gia wanted me back home by seven for dinner, we are having fried galunggong fish. By 6:15 PM, we were already done and just wanted to take aesthetic pictures since we both had on cute outfits. We left by 6:25 pm and she dropped me off at home. As I grabbed my keys and purse, she looked me in the eyes and kissed me goodbye.

COMING SOON

Goddess of Munich, Germany - October 2024

Meet Kuro - Winter 2024